OTHER TRUTHS

OTHER TRUTHS

By

Thomas Grissom

SUNSTONE
PRESS

SANTA FE

Sunstone books may be purchased for educational, business, or sales promotional use.
For information please write: Special Markets Department, Sunstone Press,
P.O. Box 2321, Santa Fe, New Mexico 87504-2321.

Printed on acid-free paper
∞

Library of Congress Cataloging-in-Publication Data

Grissom, Thomas, 1940-
  Other truths : poems / by Thomas Grissom.
    p. cm.
  ISBN 978-0-86534-884-4 (pbk. : alk. paper)
  I. Title.
  PS3607.R577O84 2012
  811'.6--dc23
                                          2012009934

WWW.SUNSTONEPRESS.COM
SUNSTONE PRESS / POST OFFICE BOX 2321 / SANTA FE, NM 87504-2321 /USA
(505) 988-4418 / ORDERS ONLY (800) 243-5644 / FAX (505) 988-1025

Perish, abhorred, the man who never brings himself to
unbolt his heart in frankness to some honored friends.
                                        Euripides, *Medea*

A guilty conscience needs to confess. A work of art
is a confession, and I must bear witness.
                                        Camus, *Notebooks*

But my guess is you will get rid of all that by writing
about it, he said. Once you write it down it is all gone.
                                Hemingway, *For Whom the Bell Tolls*

You asked how old I was? I made no verse,
but one or two, before this winter, sir.

Emily Dickinson

CONTENTS

Other Truths

Themes

What Manner of Men:
Variations on a Theme

INTRODUCTION

It was Robert Penn Warren who advised that the less a poet tries to say about his own work perhaps the better. Robert Frost expressed the same sentiment many years earlier when, in response to a request that he explain some of his poetry, he merely replied that he had said it the best he knew how in the poems themselves. These poems, too, must speak for themselves, and I shall not presume here to go beyond what I have already tried to convey in the poems. Even so, a few remarks may be fitting.

The poems included here were all written more or less during a single period of time and reflect the situation and circumstances that existed then. Each one was at the time fully as necessary as the next breath, not to be denied. Afterwards, I put them aside but never quite out of mind. On those occasions when I went back to read them again, I was always dismayed to realize how little each of them seemed to say of all that I had felt and needed to say at that moment. In spite of the fact that there had been no conscious intent to go beyond writing a few poems during the time they were written, I began to look for arrangements by which taken all together they would more nearly convey my meaning than any of the poems individually could do. To my surprise and delight I found that there was indeed a quite natural arrangement in keeping with the thoughts and emotions that gave rise to these poems. And when they were viewed in this broader context a natural theme emerged. This little book is the result.

A poem written at the same time but not included here began with the lines

> *If all were known and truth were told*
> *They are more for me than you these lines*
> *That say what's on my mind . . .*

What was true of those lines is equally true of all these poems. They were not written with the thought of anyone else ever reading them. They are poems from the heart, written truly and honestly. Poems that never seek to deny the reality of those other, darker truths of our existence. Yet not in anger or out of any sense of hopelessness or despair, but openly and truthfully with always the abiding conviction that these poems should "tell no lies." What truths they may speak I will let the poems themselves tell.

What is it that compels us always to try to express ourselves, and in so doing repeatedly risk exposing our innermost vulnerabilities to the probing scrutiny that no matter how sympathetic and understanding is nonetheless threatening and filled with apprehension? Perhaps the closest anyone can ever come to a simple answer is love, the love that binds each of us to the rest of humanity, in which no matter how desperate the circumstances we continually discover a bit of ourselves. It is in that spirit that I would have you regard any harshness you may hear in these lines.

Albuquerque, March 1983

First light was cloaked in ashen skies
My mood at dawn the same
By noon the world beamed bright and clear
My joy echoed its fame.

Then afternoon fell gray once more
Its somber tones oppressed
But twilight found me well content
To greet my final rest.

I Was Going to Write a Poem. . . .

HIDDEN DREAMS

I dreamed a poem unwritten
In thoughts that lay unborn
Conceived in troubled sleep
Dispersed by light of morn;
Then struggled through the day
To find those thoughts once more
Unable to recall
The paths I'd walked before;
And truths that night concealed
From day's bright scrutiny
Stay hidden in my mind
To shape my destiny.

THOUGHTS ARE POEMS

I was going to write a poem
Out of words that never came
And the thoughts that I was thinking
Just fell like April rain
To be soaked up by the garden
Of memories in my mind
Where they nurture other thoughts
That I will use another time. . . .

TAKEN BY SURPRISE

I keep a pad and pencil
To record my random thoughts;
Sometimes the words won't come at all;
They must not be forced, you see,
But coaxed with tender care;
It is a sort of lover's game;
And when they do come flowing out
To say just what I meant
I am the most surprised of all.

THE WINDOW IN MY MIND

The window in my mind
Opened briefly on the world
And for a fleeting moment
The truth shone brightly in
And was recorded somewhere
In my deepest memories;
Then some time much, much later
While I was dreaming thoughts
That window opened wide
And truth shone out again.

REASONS

It was something that you said
That made me write those lines,
Or perhaps some long forgotten thought,
Or just something that I felt,
Or maybe even none of these;
Still there was a world of truth
Captured in those simple lines—
No matter that I can't recall
Now how it came to be.

FADED IMAGES

There are no pretty pictures
On which to put these words,
No scenes with which to make them
More pleasing to your eye,
Only the words themselves
With whatever thoughts and images
They create in your mind—
To replace now forgotten ones
That once I had in mine.

SIMPLE PLEASURES
(Sunday Afternoon)

I write simple words
in simple lines
on yellow scraps of paper.
Does some truth
come peeking through these thoughts,
or does it even matter?
Is there something here
that might not be said
unless I took the time,
or do I just record
what others all may know
and waste the time
I could have had for living?
But then,
what would living be
without these simple pleasures
of the mind?

EFFORTS

It's what you have to say
            that counts
                        not how you say it
but how you try
            the tear stains
                        and the hurt and pain
the sunless days
            of clouds and rain
                        except when writing poems
that no one ever reads
            then it's the crumpled pages
                        on the floor
and words
            that come no more
                        images
drifting far offshore
            and thoughts
                        that fail to soar
to show
            what no one
                        ever sees
to say
            what no one
                        ever knows
but me.

REAL DEATH

Physicians of the world
              debate
                        when death occurs
with electrical impulses
              from the heart
                        and brain; but
this is only
              biological death—
                        real death
is of the mind and soul
              and often
                        comes much sooner.

CREATIVITY

The physical things of life
        can be hurried—
                but those of
mind and soul
        take time;
                creativity
follows no schedule
        appearing unannounced
            and always
with surprise.

GIFTS

The things I have most
      to give in life
            are just
my thoughts
      and hopes
            and feelings—
things of mind
      and soul
            and spirit; these
are fragile
      precious gifts
            so easily damaged
in the giving.

MY ONLY TREASURES

Do not ridicule
        my thoughts
                or mock my
deepest feelings;
        these are my only
                treasures—
all I know
        of honesty
                and truth
of beauty, faith
        and courage—
                I owe no one
the right
        to hold them up
                to scorn.

And I Just Needed to Tell You. . . .

It's the little things
      that make a love—
Things you never miss
      until they're gone—
And never know they're yours,
Until you turn
        and find they're not....

Loneliness—
stabs deepest at first thrust,
yet looms anew at each encounter,
a dark, shadowy stranger
lurking on the edge of crowds,
where the warming sounds of laughter fade—
first from memory,
and then from the heart....

ALONE

i)

Alone
is a state of mind—
before
I was alone
amidst the talk
and laughter
yet no one knew
but me—
and I did not know why.

ii)
Together then
      and yet we were alone—
           apart now
we are still alone—
      but now without each other
         to share
at least the things
      which made us
        grow apart.

iii)
This one small room
           holds all I own—
                       some clothes
a few books
           and these simple words
                       I write; I do not
count myself poorer
           for the things
                       now missing except
for two—
           the love we had
                       and the lives we shared.

SHADES OF BLUE

i)   Azure blue
bright desert skies
shimmering tears
in sad blue eyes
august now has come and gone
with april, june and july
but the sadness in my heart
still lingers on and on....

ii)   Sunrise and sunset
And all the times between
Slowly pile upon each other
To make my days now seem
Like endless hours of torture
That creep so slowly by
While I wrestle with my thoughts
About the countless reasons why.

iii)   There are clouds in the sky
That block the sun
Casting shadows on the mountains
Since you've gone
And days that are an endless string
Of hours dragging by
As I sit and contemplate
The complicated reasons why.

DEFINITIONS

i) Being alone
    is being ignored
    having thoughts
    with no one to tell them to
    and no one to care
    even if they knew;

ii) being unimportant
     to those whose opinions
     once mattered
     and trying to find the strength
     to believe in yourself
     through it all;

iii) having everything good
      you ever did
      forgotten
      and only the wrong
      remembered and recalled
      whenever you are mentioned;

iv) being blamed
     for everything
     that's wrong with life
     and searching every motive
     of everything you do
     to rid yourself of guilt;

v) knowing that the past
   went wrong
   and is gone
   and cannot be undone
   and only the future remains
   and can never be the same.

vi) Being alone
   is being trapped
   inside your mind
   with no way out
   and no way back
   to join the world.

ALL THE LONELY PEOPLE

The world is filled with people
Who eat alone in silence
Living lives overflowing
With the solitude of self
No pleasures but whatever
They can do alone
No companions but the thoughts
They think themselves
In perspectives twisted and distorted
By the loneliness they feel
Who walk the streets unsmiling
Passing by without acknowledgement
The burdens of their lonely lives
Etched deeply on the faces
Of once joyful, smiling children
As if living out a life that stretched
Beyond what should have been
Staring blankly into what the future holds
With eyes in which once burned
The bright, exuberant fires of youth
Where now one only sees
The cold, dull stares of boredom
Trudging forth against the crush
Of a life devoid of meaning
Whose purpose was fulfilled
In an earlier, happier time
And cannot be recaptured now
If purpose there ever was
In numbers overwhelming

In numbers too depressing
Struggling to postpone
The final solace of the end.

DREAMS

Everywhere—
people wearing T-shirts
proclaiming things they cannot do
and things they cannot be
yet wearing dreams upon their chests
for all the world to see
as though simple proclamation
could somehow make it be.

But lives are lived by dreams—
written clearly on the faces
and mirrored in the eyes,
etched deeply into furrowed brows
and onto wrinkled skin—
good dreams and bad alike.

SAND CASTLES

Sculptured castles on the beach
Speak of dreams beyond our reach
Built to while away the time
Adrift on seas of thoughts sublime
Fashioned from the crumbling sands
By the toil of mortals' hands
Before we turned our backs on God
And chose the paths that man has trod.

CARING IS

I don't know—
         I honestly don't;
                but I think
and feel
         and believe;
                knowing
isn't important
         to me anymore—
                caring is.

SCHIZOPHRENOS

I have forgotten what I am—
Uncertain I ever knew—
And I search in vain for meaning
Among all I thought was true;

A future ripe with promise
Has escaped into the past;
Each moment slips by fearful
That the next might be my last;

I reach and grope for comfort
That is only found within
To find my faltering efforts
Always reflected back again;

This drama forms the essence
Of the childhood times of me
And life's most threatening puzzle
Of what could and would I be.

UNKNOWN ROADS

As I drive along these unknown roads
The cars all seem to swerve and vie
To get around and pass me by,
With drivers impatient of one (such as I)
Who does not seem to know his way.
It is the same, also, for me
Along life's unfamiliar paths
As the lonely hours of each day
And the silent seasons slip away
Impatient to be done with one
For whom each change is a thing so slow
That he doesn't seem to know his way
Or even where he meant to go.

PUZZLES

Can I be quite as bad
as you have led me
to believe?
Could anyone,
ever?
If not,
why would you think so?

And if you're right
why can't I see
it too,
or are we looking
at different pieces
of the same puzzle?

All the pieces will be needed
to solve the riddle;
not one can be hoarded
if we would ever know
the truth.

If any piece is missing
it will not
be found
by looking
in the dark,
or made to fit
in the puzzle
upside down.

The greatest danger
is that one of us
will tire of this game
before the puzzle
is complete,
or see just enough
of it unfinished
to guess
the ending wrong.

As I recall
we never were
very good
at puzzles.

JUST PASSING BY

I saw you in the park
soaking up the sun
and casting shadows
on the grass,
only one of many
yet different and the fairest
and the only one
of which I had any need.

When again I looked
and found that you were gone
the sun had set
among the clouds,
and I was relieved to find
you had no need of me.

OTHER LOVERS

Before when you loved
I wonder
did you do the things
with him
that you do so well
with me?

Did he writhe the way
I do
and hold you where
I touch?

Did he take the time
to make you feel
the way
I have
and think of you
as much as of himself?

Was he as good
for you
as you have made
me think
that I must be?

And did you tell
him so
and sing his praises

in his ear
and to the bedroom walls?

And was he kind
when it was over
and did he say
that you
were just as good
as all the others
he had known?

If so
then I just wish
I might have sat
in a corner of the room
and watched you
making love to him—
with your bodies
intertwined
and your emotions
all laid bare.

It would have been
like watching me
drinking
at your fountain
of youth.

THE MORNING GLORY

A morning glory shyly placed
By one whose heart her mind outpaced
Has graced my desk for a day this year
And brought my heart much welcomed cheer.

—Near end of day the closing began
Proceeding at first according to plan
Then during the night nature resigned
This time according to man's design—

The morning glory you gave to me
No more a beautiful flower will be,
But the thought that plucked it from the vine
Will mellow with age like yesterday's wine,

To bloom in memory with the passing days
A tender reminder of mysterious ways
That nature schemes to disguise from man
All but a fragment of the master plan.

TIME MACHINES

At the end
            of running ten
                        or maybe fifteen
miles every
            mirrored image shows
                        reflections
of yourself
            in ten or maybe
                        fifteen
years. To recapture
            how I felt
                        ten or fifteen
years before
            needs but one
                        brief moment in
the shelter of
            your arms
                        worshipping
at your fountain
            of youth. Within
                        those total spans
of time stretch
            worlds enough for
                        me—
remembering the
            days and nights
                        we've had—
dreaming of
            all those
                        yet to be.

THE MAN ON THE BEACH

I met him on the beach one night,
At a time when friends were few,
Soon after I had finished running
As he walked his dog along the shore:
"I like those shoes you have my friend,"
Was the way in which he greeted me
And marked himself as one who knew
Something of what running is about.
A full, red beard and long, red hair
Pulled back and tied behind his head
Were of his features all that I could see;
Yet there was a warmth in his voice
The darkness could not hide,
That came through just as clearly
As the way the dog beside him
Shook all over as he wagged a shaggy tail.
He talked of running for a while
As only one who knows it well could do
And of how he soon would get
Another pair of shoes like mine
And take up where he left off once before,
But most of all how he was glad
That I was running on the beach
And that our paths had chanced to cross.
At length we finally parted
And he disappeared into the night
Walking with his dog along the shore.
I stood and watched him go his way,
A friend I had not known I had,

At a time when friends were few,
With no reason for being my friend
Other than he simply wanted to.

AND I JUST NEEDED TO TELL YOU
(the morning after)

Love, timeless love, and the drifting flow of eternal
    time sweeping over all
Weigh more heavily upon my mind today than usual
As I strive to understand. The need for quiet conversa-
    tion with myself
Is greater now than most: to explain what is wrong:
Why life is such a bitter cup; and the folly of the flawed
    and tragic human race
Whose worst deeds are done by hands dripping blood,
    whose
Most heroic bear still the scars of infantile egotism
    and the sullied stains
Of motives born in the dark of night. And talking
    myself
Is empty, the echoes reflected from my thoughts
    garbled with the same
False and egocentric compulsions for which I take the
Human race to task; because the only truth is love—
    unphysical, emotional—
The simple caring of one of us for another for reasons
    deep
And unfathomable as the inscrutable things I have
    been struggling to comprehend,
With always the ever longing need to reach out and
    share,
To commune and communicate with all of humanity
    by groping to touch, to grasp

Another heart and feel the glowing warmth against the
　　　　　numbing chill of life—
And I just needed to tell you.

TO DIANA

The relationship of man
and woman tenuous
at best

at worst precarious
was in the case
of you

and me the only source
of my salvation
amidst

the perils of extinction
such distinction
should

not go unheralded in a
world of failures
we were

one of the success
stories of the
age.

TO K.L.

Musing thoughtfully while
reflecting inward for some
outward expression of the
future in the presence of a
past seen through eyes that
window a mind groping
equally backward and forward
from within ever recurring
cycles of seasons impressed in
fading sights and sounds
upon memories of lives
intertwined to be no more
nor less than what they
have been and will be
within the reality of an
existence chiseled with the
more delicate reality of
essence to fashion hopes
and promises for a
future and understand what
has been and will be and
extract what we perceive of
truth and can discover of
happiness from the cycles of
our existence by reliving
events of our past lives
i am moved to rejoice in
the miracle of your birth

the joys of your life and
my hopes for your future.

Other Truths

THE RUNNER

There is beauty and a joy in the solitary form
gliding smoothly through the open countryside
in strides paced by the beat of silent, cushioned feet
to the measured rhythm of each passing mile;
the rise and fall of labored breath
the pounding heart and easy flow of sweat
sharpening an acute awareness
of a heightening physical-mental state,
creating thoughts where none were there before,
in sharper focus than the mind alone can do,
with a boldness and a clarity unattained in quieter
    times,
as the poetry of the soul flows rushing through the mind
and opens up a crystal window on the world
through which to catch a glimpse of truths as yet
    unknown.

OTHER TRUTHS

The mind seeks beauty in all the eyes behold
And listens for the truths that nature told—
Yet pauses for a moment now and then
Before a truth it cannot comprehend:
Sees the hurtling falcon's murderous plunge;
Hears the snarling leopard's deadly lunge;
Feels the numbing wastes of frozen lands;
Smells the bloated death in desert sands;
Finds it in the anguished cries of man
Shackled to his fleeting mortal span,
Driven by his consciousness to try
To fathom multitudes of reasons why—
Then wonders why a God who made the beauty
Would make these other truths so hard to see.

HELEN

Is this that which launched a thousand ships
And drew the mighty Greeks to Ilium's shore;
For ten years stirring clash of arms across
The Trojan Plains to end old Priam's line;
Inspiring the epic strains of Homer's verse
Creating for all times the sounds of poetry?
These sagging withered breasts are hardly fit
To succor worms. The wrinkled skin, the faded
Hair betray no echoes of the past.
Now only death desires these barren loins
That once lured lovers to the nuptial couch
And promised nights that time could never dim.
No, this creased and aging form now palsied
And enfeebled is not what stirred men's passions
And compelled the poet to sing. This is just
An empty shell, the debris of a life
Whose essence lies beyond the faded past;
This is but the blunted instrument
That carved a scratch on anonymity.

AFFIRMATION AND DEDICATION

He locked his heart in a silver box
And wrapped his mind in golden chains
And placed them on the altar
Of a grand and stately church;
Beneath the years of fear and gloom,
Beside the mouldy, mildewed pages
Of the greatest story ever told
And the world's all-time best seller;
Sheltered from the anguish and the torment
        of the ages
Muffled by the thick stone walls and the sounds
        of sacred hymns
Sung by souls in praise of God created
        in their image;
In a place where the sun never shines,
Where the soft, spring winds never blow;
In a place where nothing happens at all.

REFLECTIONS

Brooding deep within himself
He views the landscapes of his mind
And sorts out childhood memories
From scenes of harsher times;

And hears the peals of laughter
That swept those sunlit plains
Fade from the grasp of memory
Replaced by cries of pain;

As did the child become the man
So changed his world along the way
Transformed from brightest colors
To shades of somber gray;

Until at last the darkness
Engulfs him all around;
His eyes close for the last time;
He hears no further sound;

But embarked on his last journey
To rest beneath the sod
He leaves it now to others
To contemplate a God.

CAMELOT—THE IMPOSSIBLE DREAM
(RFK)

I recall with grief the moment when the bullet struck
    him down
With its snapping, frightening, sickening, fateful,
    prophesying sound
That dashed his hopes with ours a crumpled heap upon
    the ground;
The chaos and the tumult of the startled, swirling crowd
Drowning out the promised hopes of what might still
    have been
In the numbing realization of what now would never be;

—Somewhere in the land a lady said with dirgeful glee,
    "Well, that will make an honest man of him."—

        She spoke for all those honest men
        Who hate and seethe and loathe
        And fight to keep us free
        To murder dreams and dreamers
        Of visions yet to be.

ROBINSON JEFFERS

Old Jeffers was right, spreading his measured
                prophesies of doom
Brisk and chilling as the sea winds that sweep the
                coastal peaks,
Sharp and craggy as the granite cliffs he loved,
Gentle as the verdant mantle of a rich and fertile earth
Or the salt sea spray of waves cascading on a
                moonlit shore,
Winged with wisdom, soaring higher than the hawk
Gazing disinterestedly down upon the fierce
                consciousness
Peering earthward, oceanward, skyward for the truths
                that sustained and nurtured his art.
No matter that the apocalypse is yet to be:
There is time enough, and time is but a blink
Of the eye of the hawk and generations of hawks to
                come,
But a fleeting thought in the consciousness of man.
It is near enough: man lives perched on the precipice
                of his doom
Oblivious to his mortality and impermanence, blinded
                by
His feeble consciousness to the realization he, too,
Lives and perishes by the same laws as the hawk
And needs to be reminded; to hear in the roar of
                surging seas
Crashing impotently at the feet of granite cliffs,
Unscarred since long before the poet first stood and
                peered westward,

The echoes of his own precariousness, the measures
of his fragility.
No matter that the doom he sensed may never be
completed:
It is with us always, inexorably wearing and shaping
humanity
Even as the seas weather the granite cliffs, crumbling
one by one
The foundations of mighty civilizations as empire
replaces empire
To fuel the sacrificial altar fires of progress,
greed and avarice.
No matter that he is no longer with us: for
He left us his poetry and a vision of truth and
wisdom
Reaching far enough ahead to where another poet
Will someday climb the lonely paths that mount those
solid, granite cliffs
And stand where Jeffers stood, gazing fiercely westward
Like a hawk perched at the pinnacle of man's last
refuge,
And once more fashion verse to remind us of his truths.

THE POETRY AND THE BIRDS

The poetry and the birds: that's all there really is;
All else is but illusion, the senseless games of
        simple minds
Blinded by the glare of false grandeur, too human
        for permanence.
Homer knew it three thousand years ago on the shores
        of the Aegean,
And we know it still in a thousand translations of
        his words,
Of the deeds of men to be sure, but always as the
        playthings of the Gods
With mortal finish even to the mightiest. Euripides
Peered deeper still, unwrapping man from the enfolding
        embrace of the Gods,
Exposing an image: crude, imperfect, unfinished,
        which generations of poets
Have hewn and crafted and refined, until on the
        precipice of his doom
Man stands naked and exposed for what he is:
        insignificant, puny, impermanent,
Precariously balanced on the knife edge of existence;
        yet for all that
A cunning and clever animal lacking only wisdom,
        whose consciousness
Blinds him to the realization he answers to the same
        laws as the hawk.
The hawk knows it even if man does not; with calm
        dignity and fierce aloofness

His undaunted eyes peer down upon the ruins of
            civilizations, awaiting only
To reclaim his kingdom from the pillage of the
            conscious intruder.
Man uses his cleverness to soar with the birds even
            to the very
Threshold of spreading his seed on the celestial winds
            of the universe,
Like the spore of a dying organism reaching out
            for new life,
Only to crash in the carnage of his own senselessness
Where the birds will look down upon the broken,
            bleeding corpse
Then fly away to greet the next great race of poets.

ANTIQUE TRUTHS

I stopped by the antique fair
To reminisce and view the wares,
Every object old and worn,
The luster gone that time had shorn,
The only test for being there
The toll of years that each had borne,
No concern at all for usefulness
Then or now—junk some might call it—
Yet not exactly junk somehow
To those who came to look and learn
What antique truths they could discern
In peering safely back through time
And holding firmly to the grasp
Of the certainty of the past.

THE TURKISH BOW

I paid a hundred dollars once
For a bow that shot a half a mile
Crafted by the bowyer Drake
With curves that leered like a Turkish smile;
Made of wood and glass and glue
In place of animal horn and sinew
Its limbs recurved in sweeping bends
And overlaid tips with half moon ends;
A gleaming handle of metal and wood
Cradled my hand as no leather grip could;
A dacron string very delicate and light
Propelled the arrow on its distant flight
With a start so sudden it was lost from sight
And couldn't be seen when the shot was made right.
The arrows were the slenderest of needles
Exactly one Turkish unit of length
The finest ever fashioned by arrowsmith Denton
From Port Orford Cedar of singular strength;
Cut from the wood of Ulrich Number Nine,
A log of cedar grained straight and fine,
With plastic nocks and shining brass piles
And fletched with tiny plastic vanes
To guide each true for half a mile.
I shot it once to learn its truths
That spoke from down through ages past
When Turkish archers used such bows
To cast their arrows far and fast,
And felt the spirit of Effendi
Standing right there at my side

As he watched each shot I made
Fail to match his best with pride;
And then I hung it on my wall
Not to chance that I might mar
Two thousand years of perfect knowledge
Of how to shoot an arrow far.

WHEN KNOWING STOPS

Wisdom is not caused to be by reaching
Out to seize and hold it in our grasp
The way we would a piece of land or something
Else we own as just a part of living;
Nor can we ever be as sure of it
As of the wind and earth and sky
Or always find it in our view the way
We gaze upon the beauty of a tree;
It eludes our grasp forever
And slips always out of reach
When we try to own it for ourselves
And put it on display;
By giving it away we find it;
By denying it is ours does it
Come to serve us when we need it;
Wisdom starts when knowing stops
And questioning becomes the thing we do.

TEACHING THE CHILDREN

It is too bad, he said,
that we have to make a child
feel like he is a failure
by expecting him to do
more than he can by then,
instead of just enjoying
the things that he can do
and telling him how well he's done
and how he should feel proud.

It is too bad, he said,
to leave him with the feeling
that in spite of all himself
he has put into a thing
it still wasn't good enough
and that he didn't measure up
but somehow let us down.

We who have no right to live
our lives again in his
but yet to please ourselves
we ask him to be more
than he was ever meant to be
and rob him of the joy
of that early part of life.

And when in later years
his life becomes a task
and he must struggle with himself

to grasp at more than he can reach
then must he also fear again
that he will only fail
and miss whatever chance
he might have had to win.

It is too bad, he said,
that we teach our children thus
to fear the spectre of defeat,
instead of finding there a chance
to play the game again
and repeat all the fun they missed
when first the thing was done;
to keep the game alive
until they chance to find a way
to make the ending somehow
come out all right at last,
as a thing not ever to be feared
but expected at the end.

It is too bad, he said,
that these children grow to be
ourselves who fear defeat as well
and fearing it we always seek
to keep from out its path
and never take the risks
that shield us from success.

Yes, it is too bad, he said,
and in my heart and mind I knew

from the child that lives in each of us
that what he said was true.

THE OLD FOLK

They are old folk
and they are innocent
and blameless of any guilt
for the sins of the past
and the shortcomings we now see
in ourselves and in the world
and the people all around us.

They did what they did
innocent of any harm
which they wrought on the future,
unaware of how a single act
or even one whole lifetime
would appear time and again
to leave its imprint on the future.

Their time is past
and we cannot now blame
our problems and frustrations
on them who went before us
to escape the blame ourselves.

Their deeds are done and finished
and must be accepted
as the place where we will start
to make a future of our own.

There is not one problem
that ever can be solved
by railing at past sins
and not one that can withstand
the innocence of the future.

Let us take the love they gave
and forgive the love withheld
and weave it in our lives
to build the future on,
for there were none among them
who did not yearn to love,
only some for whom
love seemed to pass them by.

ALL THE WORLD'S A POEM

"There is one God and the Earth is His prophet."
— Robinson Jeffers

All the world's a poem
Printed on the earth
Where God the Poet writes
With majesty His verse

In the splendid truths
That simple nature told
To minds that search for beauty
In all the eyes behold;

And when a verse obscure
We strive to understand
Seek the final meaning
Within the mind of man;

For if unconvinced
Why each verse is true
At least we can be certain
That the Poet knew.

CYCLES

Rolling wave on rolling wave
Comes tumbling into shore
Booming loudly o'er the land
The sea's majestic roar.

Driven on by wind and wave
And calmed at last by land
The mounting seas come surging forth
To crash upon the sand.

Muffled murmurings of long ago
When life began beneath the sea;
Distant sounds from ages past
And of things still yet to be.

Written in this ageless cycle
Summarized for all to know
Is the essence of the universe
And nature's endless flow.

THE LAST WHOOPING CRANE
(At Bosque del Apache)

He stalks among the sandhills
a relic from the past;
his solitary presence,
a portent for the future,
marks him now the last
of a species perched precariously
on the edge of extinction
as the passenger pigeon
and the ivory bill before,
soon to be a footnote
in a text on evolution.
The ghost white form goes gliding
through the reeds along the marsh
spearing fish in the shallows
like a prehistoric savage,
one bright eye always cocked
and intent upon the prey,
the wind gently rustling
the delicate feathery spray,
water dripping from the beak
sending ripples through the pond
like memories of times gone by
when other whoopers waded there.
Who knows what is lost
when at last he is no more;
can we measure it,
and how could we ignore
his going till that time

when by then it was too late
to register any change
in the species' final fate?
They are but empty questions,
more than we can comprehend,
this measure of the meaning
of a life form's final end.

THE COTTONWOODS

Gnarled gaunt gargantuan
trunks upholding
massive mangled limbs
ghost demons of the dawn
arms outstretched to graying skies
       beseeching bloody sunsets
       bathed by summer thunderstorms
       wrapped in ermine winter cloaks
       shimmering green in prairie winds
       spreading softly brown and yellow blankets
       alongside desert streams
the mighty groves of cottonwoods
bosques
       where the haze of ancient fires
       lingers in the dawn
       with spirits of the ancient ones
       anasazi
waiting patiently to greet the future races
       the foolishness of the present age
       no more then
       than the memory now
       of anasazi
patrician prophets of the indifferent God
the trees
       bend in the wind
       sicken and die
       burnt and blackened by prairie fires
       betrayed by the thinking animals

yet arms outstretched
to distant dawns
the trees
endure.

THE FLOCK

The gulls
swarming, swirling
shrieking, shrilling
turning, twisting
twining, throbbing
probing, prying
pressing, pulsing
a raucous chorus of cacophonous cries
frantic pleadings of urgent expectancy
a swelling cloud of white on blue
rising from the beach
like dancing scraps of paper
swept aloft on sudden gusts
flapping, floating
flaring, fluttering
sweeping, swooping
settling, standing
facing squarely in the wind
staring calmly at the sea
preening, peering
passive, patient
the gulls.

BROWN PELICANS

How decidedly and in what determined
Unison they sweep silently by scarcely
Beyond the reach of the thrusting treetops the
Palms that mutely line the beach,
Serpentlike but majestic nevertheless and
Graceful with considerable skill at flying—
Skimming effortlessly alone or in formation
The calm surface of the water trading
Stingy inches of altitude for motionless wings,
Climbing upward on laboring wingbeats
To suddenly dive a folded projectile
Head first beneath the waves and
Reappear pouch bulging with fish.

BLACK ON WHITE

A mushroom cloud

keeps forming in my brain
to fill

the night sky with
the brilliance of a burning

passion
or a blinding

flash of insight into
darker

truths unyielding
to the duller light of

reason
shining down

through the ages on the
blackness

of our souls.

POINT OF VIEW

The Poets: the Poets lie too much—Thus Spoke Zarathustra

I would that I had written my poems
Or even one
Than all else I have done in life
Or left undone;

And I would have been troubled by life
Than to have sailed complacently through
For nights still separate the days
And thorns will grow where roses do.

I would that I thought bitter thoughts
Or one or two
Than all the sweeter things in life
I didn't do;

For I have come by that to know
Much more of truth than I redeem
From all the pleasantries of life
That never are quite what they seem.

IMMORTALITY

The desert skies will be my shroud
Its sands will clothe my bones
Its birds will sing me lullabies
When fore'er it is my home;

And I will lie deep in its quiet
While immortal time drifts by
As the universe unfolds each night
In the starlit desert sky;

My atoms linked with all that's been
And all that's yet to be
Will serve me well enough, I think,
For immortality.

Themes

THEMES

This farm
this longed for land
sheltered deep in Tennessee
shelters me
like every friend I ever had
or God Himself.

A place where all the world's
a poem
printed on the earth
in the transhuman beauty of things
where God the Poet writes His verse
with tender majesty
in simple truths that nature told
to minds that search for beauty
in all the eyes behold.

Where yellow poplars loom
like silent sentinels
with oak and pine and elm
holding up the sky
from feet placed firmly in the soil
standing guard along the fencerows
keeping woods away from pastures
building shelter walls
for those truths that lie within
good fences to make good neighbors
out of God and men.

An asphalt stream
its surface frozen solid
even on the hottest day
flows down these hills and valleys
to the cities far away
an umbilical cord to safety
should any feel the need
to escape
or to return
along those unknown roads
and unfamiliar paths.

Pastures green with peace
stretched between the woodland walls
yard a farmhouse
stocked with dreams
and bitter memories
at the end
or the beginning
of a cedared lane.

Here two lonely people dwell
and eat alone in silence
amid the solitude of self
and from here I have strolled
across the landscapes of my mind
from the dreamworld of reality
into the dreamworld of the mind
debating who was right
and who was wrong
to the troubled strains

of our unharmonious song
unable to get on
with life
or with living.

Spread about the countryside
narrow roads and winding lanes
where with beauty and a joy
I have run
in strides paced by the beat
of silent cushioned feet
to the measured rhythm
of each passing mile
creating thoughts
where none were there before
in sharper focus
than the mind alone can do.

Building confidence up the hills
gliding down the backsides
like sliding down to heaven
shedding troubles like the sweat
pouring from my brow
playing hide and seek with shadows
printed on the road
and suspended in the air.

Remembering other runners
or a man on the beach
at a time when friends were few
with no reason for being my friend

other than he wanted to
and other faces glimpsed with need
while I was passing by
as I paused to contemplate
the complicated reasons why.

The little churchyard cemetery
reminding me of death
and the reflections of a mind
sorting childhood memories
from scenes of harsher times
hearing peals of laughter
sweeping sunlit plains
fade from grasp of memory
replaced by cries of pain
to thoughts of lack of fear
when final death is near
and thoughts of being part
of all that's yet to be
under shrouds of desert skies
wrapped in immortality.

Composing fragile gifts of thought
through windows in my mind
poems for me for you
simple pleasures of the mind
thoughts for me to give
to try and tell you all the reasons
that don't matter any more
and that I can't recall

the simple products of a life
that are all I have to give.

Surprised by the appearance
of creativity unannounced
peering back around to see
where I've been
and where I'll be
against the unknown of a future
closing on me fast
paying attention to detail
against those forces that determine
if we succeed
or if we fail.

Solving puzzles in the dark
from pieces upside down
dreaming poems
that go unwritten
out of words
that never come
to escape from being alone
with no way back
to join the world
and elude for yet a while
that other death
the real death
of the heart and mind and soul.

There stands the ancient antique barn
filled with objects old and worn

the luster gone that time has shorn
objects now of antique truths
by peering safely back through time
and holding firmly to the grasp
of the certainty of the past.

There the shade of sugar maple
where I sat and watched the birds
the hawks high overhead
and wrote those poems
about old Jeffers
and his poetry and the birds
rock solid themes and true
and where Helen spoke to me
through moods of absurdity
of scratches left on anonymity.

I have dreamed these thoughts before
been all these things and more
in the shelter of this farm
and been less
by all that I want not to be
in the solace of this land
sheltered deep in Tennessee.

What Manner of Men:
Variations on a Theme

When the voices spoke to me
I listened—
While the words went on the paper
Time stood still—
Immersed in the noises of crowds
There was only silence—
And all the pain I ever felt
Was worth it....

THE POLITICIAN AND THE AGING ACTOR

The Politician greeted the Aging Actor on a stage
Shadowed by towering memorials and magnificent
         buildings of state—

Said the Politician:
I told them of the need to preserve the dignity of man,
         to strive for human rights;
To cleanse the environment for our children and to gird
         for a future of limited growth;
But they did not want to hear: to be believed
Such words must come from the mouth of a great leader.

Answered the Aging Actor:
They are greedy and do not want to know the truth;
And a nation of greedy men does not breed great
         leaders;
But they are gullible and I can act the part: tell them
What they want to hear while doing what is necessary;
Give them what they desire, and if they destroy
         themselves
At least I will glory in my last great role.

At the final curtain the two took their bows
To a standing ovation from the crowd
And glowing acclaim from the critics.

SOMETHING OF BEAUTY

When they write of us they will remember our wars
And speak of man the miserable murderer
Who in the span of half a century has murdered
        fifty millions:
Men—yes—but women too and children, the
        unforgiveable sin—
Denied the right to full measure of sweetness
        here on earth—
All the while clambering up the rotting heaps
        of bodies
To reach for the stars with his clever machines
        and seek new life to kill;
Man, whom the poets and novelists admire—
Seeing in him a certain beauty and courage,
        wisdom and heroism
Enough to balance out the folly, and they too
        are right:
Man is beautiful, but it is a deadly beauty
White hot as the sun, cold and austere as the
        distant stars,
Unforgiving and final as death itself;
What survives us will be our legacy of murder
        and destruction
For we are surely clever, but devoid of wisdom
Have created monsters threatening to devour us;
Some will write instead of our achievements
Of our skill with tools and technology and of
        our thirst for discovery

And overlook the smoldering ruins from which
        new civilizations rise;
For the poets and novelists speak truth: man
        will indeed survive
And possesses the pitiful capacity to find in
        the misery of his condition
Always something of beauty.

NO MORE BIG WARS

Wars—big wars—having been made at last too terrible
Little wars will serve to slake the human blood lust;
Man hungering after knowledge but with thirst
                quenched by discovery
Has bottled the primordial fires threatening now to
                warm the earth and burn away
The encrusted filth and corruption of civilizations.
Prometheus knew not these flames nor ever intended
                them
To flicker shadows across man's hearth;
Man fears them wisely but finds not wisdom in his fears
Storing instead the bottled demons in temples of
                darkness—
Hidden against the day of unleashing—
Content the while to use old tools to kill in moderation.
It is the unhealed wound in the brain—echoes of our
                ancient savagery—
The Caucasian arrogance of superiority—
That leads meanwhile the Jew and Arab, black and
                yellow man
To the playgrounds of death at the bidding of the fairer
                haired brother.
Man the discoverer may yet one day grow bored and
                weary of limited murder and
Having failed to find elsewhere the wisdom he seeks
Uncork the magic plutonium flasks of deuterons
To light the darker recesses of the human spirit
And search for it there as the moth the flame;

Until then—and ever after—there will be no more big wars.

WHAT DESERVING IRONY

Malathion, parathion, guthion: names like miching
        mallecho;
Endrin, aldrin, dieldrin: twentieth century nectars of
        the gods of greed and gluttony;
Toxaphene and DDT: elixirs of the modern alchemy of
        life into death—
Broken rings and tattered chains of hydrocarbon bonds,
        the basic molecules of life,
Distilled from the muck and ooze of living things long
        dead,
Mixed with the stuff of excrement and old bones then
Brewed in chlorine vapors and the sulphurous fumes of
        hell's own brimstone fires
To poison and pollute the earth: to deny nature that
        man might exceed his share—
Unmindful ever that man but reaps that which he sows
And cannot escape his fate. Handled carelessly long ago
Such toxin residues are yet within these cells to threaten
        death:
What deserving irony to face the fate that may befall
        all life—
To mirror in one's own demise that which may someday
Cleanse the earth of man and leave the solitary insect's
        song
To serenade each setting sun.

IMMORTALITY OR ABSURDITY

The thinking apes descended the trees onto the plains
And struggling to survive discovered fire and tools—
The shaper of man's consciousness from which sprung
        imagination and creativity;
Triumphant at last in the struggle for survival, the
        instincts lingered,
Triggering the unceasing quest for understanding—
This the grim contest where man is outwitted
And failing has used imagination to invent Gods,
These having tempted him with immortality;
Fear born of his failures holds him to his myths
Though he can but shrink in shame at what he is
As measure of one destined and deserving of such
        sweet gifts:
Founder of empires consecrated in blood,
Worshipping the false prophets of progress, man
Writes his history in cunning and ruthless ambition
Upon a legacy of deceit, destruction and murder;
Once the center of the universe today he stands
        bewildered and
Dazed by the deaths of millions in two great wars—
Now has captured suns but cannot control them and
        knows they breed a third;
Recognizing himself a puny, insignificant creature,
        the product of chance,
Adrift alone on a speck in this galaxy,
In a universe of a hundred billion galaxies
Destined to expand forever to nothingness or shrink
        back into oblivion,

No longer able to comprehend even that which he
   knows as truth,
Looks again at himself and sees written on the face
   of his fears—
Not immortality but absurdity.

WHAT MANNER OF MEN

What manner of men are these that ascended mountains
    to sit at the feet of the sun
And worshipping there discovered secrets of primordial
    fires on earth
Brighter than a thousand suns, and knew in the pleasure
    of their labor
Sin and the corruption of power, and sinning committed
    still greater sins
Betraying soul and conscience for the sweeter promise
    of discovery:
For the good of all mankind they chant—wishing to
    believe—
But will mouth anything and are not to be believed:
Man the inquisitive animal scurrying to explore each
    dark and gloomy passage
In the labyrinths of his universe, peering inward and
    outward into
The voids of infinitesimal matter and the infinite space
    of galaxies stretching
Backward and forward in time, never mindful whence
    the path,
In step to the alluring music of the mind, mesmerized
    by the illusion of progress and
Blinded by the greed for riches soon to be the shard
    heaps of future civilizations:
Man who can love women and children but himself
    more than humanity:
These not Promethean giants but merely men:

One more pitiable, insignificant process in the natural
              order of things
That is God.

ARAB VS. JEW

Overhead the roar of aircraft shattering the serenity of
        Mediterranean skies; below the rattle of
Howitzer and tank cannon scattering death across the
        plains;
Surface to air missiles streak skyward to pluck the metal
        vultures from the air;
Columns of tanks advance against the hapless foe
        amidst
The smoke and stench of napalm cleansed bones left
        rotting to bleach in the desert sun:
The sound and fury of modern man rises above these
        ancient lands of prophecy
As twentieth century pestilence settles over Israel and
        its tribal neighbors:
Arab vs. Jew: the world's proving ground for new
        technologies of limited warfare
Where East and West match armaments in tanks and
        guns, planes and missiles,
To probe the delicate balance of power, the outcome
Chiseled on the gravestones of Israeli schoolchildren
        and Palestinian mothers:
Technological man grown discontent with peace and the
        security of his civilizations,
No new worlds to conquer, craves fresh excitement and
Seeks it in the darkness and primitive savagery of battle,
Bartering lives for the grinning mockery of heroism
        and glory
Reaffirmed in senseless -ism's: nationalism and patriot-
        ism, Judaism and Muhammadanism,

116

Each side wiping blood smeared hands on the tattered
        sins of the other
Only the merchants of death lacking conscience and
        pity:
America: swelling its coffers and feeding waste and
        wantonness
With Arab oil looks away at the fresh dug graves, is
Deaf to the throttled gurgle of blood choked throats
As thousands throng each day to work and raise families
        in luxury and splendor
That Arab and Jew, women and children might die;
And who asks why: because it is written says the Jew
That the children of Abraham shall inherit these lands;
For vengeance answers the Arab and his cause is just;
It is religion, the racial flaw, the madness in men's
        minds:
And some cry Allah and some Jehovah, but all shall
        know Him as Death.

IMPERMANENCE: MANKIND'S BEAUTY

These things are beautiful: snow draped peaks purple
    hued
And thrusting to greet the sunrise above a desert dawn;
The intensity of the falcon's gaze—piercing, in-
    domitable, aloof;
Alongside desert streams ancient bosques of gnarled
    and twisted cottonwoods shimmering
Green at the touch of summer breezes, ghostly
    apparitions against the winter snow;
Goose music from an autumn sky; primordial echoes in
    the sandhill's trumpeting bugle;
Violence and renewal spawned of summer thunder-
    storms drenching desert sands, dissolving
    old limestone,
Summoning new life. And this beauty has permanence:
A reality unto itself beautiful and enduring in the eyes
    of God
With no need of man. Man on the other hand scatters
His debris across the earth: scrap heaps of rusting metal
    and crumbling stones:
Refuse from the squalor and decadence of old
    civilizations
And this too has beauty: man's beauty: impermanence;
Man's innateness and concept are beauty from which
Only his reality shrinks in shame, and man's enduring
    promise is impermanence.
I, too, do not believe in the end of man nor relish it for
    an instant
But cannot discount his capacity for mischief and folly;

Barely thirty centuries ago western civilization began
With Homer's epic poem of a bloody and fated war
              waged by men and Gods and
Could as surely end in the chronicles of equally
              ignominious and horrible holocaust.
Against this other beauty: mankind's beauty:
              impermanence.

EGOMANIA

Surrounded by the natural beauty of things—of granite
        cliffs and mountains, of pounding surf and
Desert mesas, shimmering suns and jeweled skies—
Man blinded to it perceives it not, but looking instead
        inward and finding there
A radiance more to his liking conceives his own beauty:
Egomania: enamored by the strength of his intellect and
Worshipping at the sacred shrines of science in the
        temples of technology
Man has seen his beauty flower and obscure this other
        beauty:
From Greek genius to Roman rulers; from fabled
        Byzantium to feudal Europe;
From Renaissance renewal to spread of colonial
        empires, new worlds discovered and
        conquered
As empire replaced empire, until at last westering man
        stood peering oceanward and
Looking west at his origins saw no new worlds to
        conquer;
Then turning inward directed the power of his intellect
        to knowing what he had conquered
Creating science and the symboled writing of the Gods,
Mathematics, to probe inward and outward the unseen
        voids of
Microcosm and macrocosm, finding there unity and
        ultimate beauty—serene, majestic—
Yet not wisdom or insight but only discovery from
        which he

Fashions clever tools to promulgate his beauty, spread-
        ing civilizations across the globe
Building cities and laying waste the land until he is four
        billions and challenges the
Earth itself for its riches all the while looking beyond
To the stars as if hearing inside the brain some celestial
        siren's song
Luring him onward in death's agony; with bloodied
        hands
Waging wars and finding that too beautied in heroism
        and glory, until this century
Shamed by the deaths of millions in two global wars
        and
Dreading now a third to be fought in the furied glare of
        harnessed suns
Finds himself alone and frightened in a Godless
        universe
Aware of his anguish, forelornness and despair, per-
        sistent in the conviction of his survival,
And casting about piteously for the beauty and solace
        he desperately craves sees
Finally in the leering countenance of his egomania only
The empty grinning spectre of death.

OUT OF THE CITIES AND INTO THE STARS

Huddled on these plains and in the nearby mountains
Driven in wonderment at the night skies to look
Inside himself: prehistoric man: puzzling those distant
Points of light jeweling the velvet cloak of darkness,
First knew the seasons in nameless constellations,
Felt the rhythm of moon and tides, sun and stars
Until fire, warmth, light became the soul of man;
And stirred by the flickering sparks in his brain
Nurtured the dancing red flower of fire-giver lightning
Sowing it among the people until the campfire
Sites were settlements sprawling across the plains
Transforming earth to nocturnal images of the heavens
And man's curiosity to the white heat of passion:
Capturing lightning to course the earth at his bidding;
In the furnaces of the brain forging tools hammered
And shaped on the anvil of man's inquisitiveness—
Small hands to grope inside the atom's core,
Long arms to reach and grasp at distant stars,
Tools to free the mind to quest for reasons why—
Creating gods to share the blame for failures
And assume his guilt; in these mountainous
Deserts of ancient ocean beds worshipping the
Stars in symboled languages of beauty to wrest
The secrets of cosmic fires that burn the seas,
Harnessing the sun to draw the chariots of war
Threatening now to trample and destroy him;
At last the earth subdued, his destruction threatened,
Man lies trapped within these cities, surrounded by
His kind, shackled to a legacy of death and defeat—

To once more heed the call of celestial sirens' song
And feel the forgotten lure of faintly shimmering fires
Beckon him out of the cities and into the stars.